Recycling

Charlotte Wilcox

LERNER PUBLICATIONS COMPANY
MINNEAPOLIS

Lerner Publications Company
A division of Lerner Publishing Group, Inc.
241 First Avenue North
Minneapolis, MN 55401 U.S.A.

Website address: www.lernerbooks.com

Library of Congress Cataloging-in-Publication Data

Wilcox, Charlotte.
        Recycling / by Charlotte Wilcox.
            p.   cm. — (Cool science)
        Includes bibliographical references and index.
        ISBN-13: 978–0-8225–6768–4 (lib. bdg. : alk. paper)
        1. Salvage (Waste, etc.)—Juvenile literature. 2. Recycling (Waste, etc.)—Juvenile literature. I. Title.
    HD9975.A2W55 2008
    363.72'8—dc22   2006102423

Manufactured in the United States of America
1 2 3 4 5 6 – JR – 13 12 11 10 09 08

Table of Contents

Introduction

Every year North Americans use about one hundred billion plastic shopping bags, forty billion plastic bottles, and 80 million tons (72.6 million metric tons) of paper. We use most of this stuff once, then throw it away. Cars, cell phones, and computers last longer—maybe a few years. Still, every year we junk about fifteen million cars, fifty million computers, and more than one hundred million cell phones.

Where do we put all this unwanted stuff? It's a huge problem. Leaving trash out in the open is illegal. It invites pests, spreads disease, and smells bad. Most trash goes to landfills, where workers

IT'S A FACT!

The United States makes more trash than any other country. Each American throws away an average of 4.5 pounds (2 kilograms) of garbage every day. But we also recycle more than any other country. We recycle about one-third of our trash.

bury it under dirt. The bottom of a landfill is lined with waterproof material. This keeps rotten and dangerous liquids from leaking into the environment.

New trash arrives every day, and workers add more dirt to cover it. As the trash keeps coming, workers must pile landfills higher or spread them out over more land. Over time they get too big to manage and must close.

When landfills close, cities and towns need new ones. They must be nearby so trucks don't have to haul garbage too far.

IT'S A FACT!

In one year Americans recycled:

88.9% of our used newspapers

71.5% of our used corrugated cardboard boxes

62.9% of our used steel cans

56.3% of our yard trimmings

44.8% of our used aluminum cans

38.5% of our used magazines

35.6% of our used tires

34.1% of our used plastic soft-drink bottles

28.8% of our used plastic milk and water bottles

25.3% of our used glass jars

This landfill worker is burying garbage under dirt to cover the smell and keep animals away.

It's expensive to put trash in landfills. Burying tons of trash every day takes lots of workers, machines, and fuel. Landfills take up valuable land that people could use for homes, farms, and businesses. Tossing less trash means we have less need for landfills.

Recycling is one way to keep trash out of landfills. Paper, plastic, aluminum cans, and steel car frames are some of the most often recycled

Fresh Kills Landfill

New York City's largest landfill covers about 2,200 acres (890 hectares). It's one of only a few artificial structures visible from outer space. Fresh Kills Landfill closed in March 2001 after more than fifty years of piling up trash. After the September 11, 2001, attacks on the World Trade Center in New York, Fresh Kills reopened to take the trash from the collapsed Twin Towers. Much of the trash was later recycled.

Fresh Kills Landfill is closed again for good. The city plans to turn it into a park. It will include two artificial hills. They'll be the size and shape of the World Trade Center towers laid on their sides. People can climb to the tops of the hills. From there they'll be able to see the part of New York City where the towers once stood.

At Fresh Kills Landfill, piles of debris from New York City's Twin Towers frame a view of the city's skyline.

The Recycling Circle

Collection

People collect recyclable items at homes, schools, and businesses. They take the items to collection centers, or garbage haulers pick up the items.

Processing

Recyclable trash goes to a recycling center, or materials recovery facility, for sorting and processing. Workers and machines shred, chop, or wash some materials. Machines press each type of material into bales, or tightly bound bundles.

Sale

Recycling centers sell bales to manufacturers (businesses that make things).

Manufacturing

Manufacturers use the materials to make new products. These include cloth, packaging, paper products, and building materials.

Reuse

People buy products made from recycled materials, completing the circle. Some materials, like paper and aluminum, can go around the circle several times.

items. They're mostly recycled into more of the same things. For example, used paper becomes new paper. Old aluminum cans make new aluminum cans.

People are coming up with creative new ways to recycle. These ideas turn old trash into completely different new things. For example, plastic bottles can become T-shirts. Tires can turn into floors. Rotten garbage can make energy to power homes and businesses.

Recycling turns trash into valuable resources. That's what this book is about.

chapter 1

Trashy Threads

Recycling old clothing isn't a new idea. People have been cutting up worn-out clothes to make quilts, rugs, and cleaning rags for a long time. But making new clothes out of other kinds of trash is a very new idea. It helps the environment by using things that would otherwise go in landfills. Companies make clothing, hats, shoes, and luggage from all sorts of trash.

Bottles and Jars Become Bottoms and Tops

The kind of trash that most often becomes clothing is polyethylene terephthalate (PETE). People make drink bottles and food jars from this type of plastic. We can recycle PETE into not only cloth, but also carpet and fiberfill (stuffing for jackets, sleeping bags, quilts, and pillows).

PETE usually arrives at the recycling center mixed with other plastic

This plant sorts different plastic products so they can be recycled and used again.

things. These must be sorted out. The different colors of PETE must be separated. Bottle caps and rings aren't made of PETE, so they all must come off. In many recycling centers, workers sort the plastics by hand. Some centers use X-ray or infrared sensors (tools that see differences in light that our eyes can't see) to help with sorting. Computers read information from the sensors to find even tiny bits of non-PETE material.

Next the PETE containers go into a machine that crushes them together into bales. The bales go to another place for more work. They still have some non-PETE materials in them. These include missed caps and rings, labels and glue, and small amounts of drinks or food. Workers and machines sort, wash, and dry the flattened containers.

Machines will shred the plastic in this bale *(left)* into flakes *(right)*.

When the sorting and cleaning are done, machines shred the containers to make PETE flakes. Manufacturers continue the recycling process by buying pure PETE flakes. Most PETE flakes go to cloth makers.

The most common fabric made from recycled PETE is polyester. To make polyester thread, machines force melted PETE through a spinneret. The spinneret is a tool with many tiny holes in it, like a showerhead. As the liquid plastic sprays through the holes, it forms strands. The strands dry and twist together into polyester thread.

IT'S A FACT!

Here's how many 20-ounce (0.59-liter) PETE bottles it takes to make some common fabric products:

One extralarge T-shirt: 15
One sweater: 63
Fiberfill for one
    ski jacket: 14
Fiberfill for one
    sleeping bag: 85
1 square foot (929
    square centimeters)
    of carpet: 14

Bigger holes make thicker strands, and smaller holes make thinner strands. Thicker strands make thicker thread. The thicker the thread, the heavier the cloth it makes.

Polyester thread from clear PETE can be bleached white or dyed any color. Thread from colored PETE won't bleach, so it must be dyed only dark colors. After the thread is bleached or dyed, it's ready for knitting or weaving into cloth. The cloth can become shirts, sweaters, underwear, safety vests, jackets, hats, and gloves.

A lot of polyester comes from recycled plastic. It's no surprise. Polyester from recycled PETE is exactly like polyester made from raw PETE. If the shirt you're wearing contains polyester, it may be made from recycled bottles and jars. You're keeping plastic out of landfills by wearing it.

A worker watches a machine weave recycled PETE thread into polyester fabric at this plant in Indonesia.

Nonwoven Fabric

Another kind of cloth made from recycled plastic is nonwoven fabric. Woven fabric is made by knitting or weaving threads together. To make nonwoven fabric, machines spread out thin sheets (called webs) of melted, tangled plastic strands. After the webs are cool and dry, machines roll them into sheets.

Nonwoven fabric is made like paper and looks like paper, but it's much stronger. It's almost impossible to tear, but it's easy to cut with scissors. Clothes made from it are light and comfortable. Nonwoven fabric breathes, or lets water vapor (steam) pass through it. This means people wearing it don't get too hot and sweaty. Even though nonwoven fabric breathes, it's also waterproof. No liquids can pass through it.

Many workers wear lab coats, coveralls, or aprons made of nonwoven fabric. These work clothes protect workers' regular clothes from things such as oil, grease, and paint. People who work with irritating or dangerous materials, such as insulation or poisonous

Coveralls made of nonwoven fabric, like the suit this man is wearing, can protect people who work with dangerous materials.

chemicals, wear nonwoven disposable coveralls. They throw them away at the end of the day. Nonwoven fabric clothes called scrubs protect medical workers from germs and keep germs from spreading. Doctors and nurses can throw away their scrubs after working with each patient.

Nonwoven fabric can be recycled many times. It's used for many other things besides clothes. These things include shipping envelopes, building materials, camping gear, and money.

Billboard Bags

Almost everywhere you go in North America, you see billboards. Hundreds of thousands of these huge signs line our highways. They cover our stadiums, buses, and trains.

Billboards come in different sizes. The biggest size is the most common. It's 14 feet (4.3 meters) high and 48 feet (14.6 m) wide. That's bigger than the floor of a two-car garage.

Billboards are printed on nylon cloth that won't tear. It's coated with vinyl to make it waterproof. The cloth for one billboard weighs nearly 100 pounds (45.4 kg). The printed cloth is stretched over a metal or wood frame and fastened in place.

Billboard ink is made to stay bright for up to eight years in sun, wind, and rain. Some billboard messages stay in place for that long. Others stay for just a few weeks or months.

Sooner or later, every billboard message gets outdated, and it has to come down. Instead of dumping old billboard cloth in landfills, people can recycle it to make useful products.

These bags from Relan, a company in Minnesota, are made from recycled billboard fabric.

Billboard companies give or sell their used cloth to manufacturers. The cloth is often dirty and wrinkled. Manufacturers wash and iron the cloth. Workers cut up the cloth to make tote bags, handbags, wallets, and eyeglass cases. The weatherproof cloth makes very strong bags. The vinyl coating gives the bags a shiny look.

Billboard bags usually show off bright colors, letters, words, or pictures. The letters, words, and pictures are so big that only small parts of them show on each bag. One fingernail or bottle cap picture might cover an entire tote bag or purse. People like the bold, colorful look of billboard bags. They also like to use something that would otherwise go in the trash.

More Trashy Fashions

Companies are making tote bags, handbags, and luggage out of many other kinds of trash too. One example is used truck inner tubes, the air-filled rings inside tires. Inner tubes turn into sleek black handbags, wallets, briefcases, suitcases, and belts. The bags and belts look like leather but are washable and waterproof.

Another example is sailcloth from sailboats. The sails wear out in spots, making them useless for sailing. But there's usually plenty of good cloth left to make other things. The strong fabric makes excellent tote bags. At least one company puts a label inside each of its sailcloth bags. The label tells what seas the cloth sailed in its former life.

A company in England makes purses and tote bags from old video- and audiotape. Workers knit or crochet the tape using a looped stitch. The workers also make purses from shopping bags the same way. They line the purses and bags with fabric from old clothes or sheets.

Shoes help keep trash out of landfills too. New shoes and sandals can be made from old tires and inner tubes. Because these products are made of rubber, the shoe soles are very strong and long-lasting. The rubber is comfortable to walk on. It also gives the shoes a great grip.

This bag made out of recycled video- and audiotape is made by a company in England. The company also makes products out of recycled plastic bags.

chapter 2

What to Do with Doo-doo

Some people call it poop or scat. Scientists call it excrement or feces. Farmers call it manure or dung. City workers call it sewage or sludge. Whatever you call it, you have to get rid of it every day. It piles up in places where there are lots of animals or people.

No one wants poop to pile up. It's stinky, ugly, and germy. But what can we do with all this doo-doo? People are finding clever new answers to this old question. Even though poop is garbage, it still contains nutrients and other valuable things. It can be turned into fertilizer, animal feed, energy, and other useful products.

Farm Manure Galore

For thousands of years, farmers have used animal manure to fertilize their fields. The nutrients in manure help plants grow. In the past, most farmers had small numbers of animals. They saved all the manure from

Many farmers use animal waste
to fertilize their crops.

their animals and spread it on their own fields. This helped them make the most of their farms' resources.

Modern farms are different. Many of them keep hundreds or thousands of animals in one place. The animals produce much more manure than their farms can use. The extra manure is a problem because it's not safe to just throw it away. To solve this problem, farming scientists are thinking up new ways to use manure.

Bedding, Beauty, and Breakfast

Some farms recycle their manure into animal bedding. They must dry and treat the manure to kill germs. This can be expensive, but it saves the cost of buying other bedding. Some scientists worry that too many germs remain in recycled manure bedding. They're studying this idea more to make sure manure bedding is as safe as possible.

Some cities and towns recycle manure to beautify their public spaces. They compost manure (mix it with rotted plants), and highway workers spread the compost along roadsides. Compost helps plants grow faster and stronger. The workers then plant grass, shrubs, flowers, or other plants along the roadsides.

Another use for manure is animal feed. The manure must, of course, be treated to kill germs and remove other unwanted materials before animals can eat it. Treated manure from cattle, hogs, and poultry (farm birds such as chickens and turkeys) is added to all kinds of animal feed. Not all scientists think this is safe. They worry that too many germs could survive the treatment. Other scientists believe it's dangerous to feed animal manure to the same kind of animal it came from.

From Excrement to Electricity

More and more big farms are making electricity from their manure. Electricity made from manure is good for the environment because it's renewable energy. (This means the source of the energy can be replaced. As long as there are animals, there will always be plenty of manure!) It's also good for the environment because it uses smelly, germy garbage that would otherwise just keep piling up.

Most electric plants in North America make electricity by burning coal or gas. There are two ways to make electricity from manure. One is to

IT'S A FACT!

Native Americans and pioneers in the central plains of North America in the 1800s burned dried dung for cooking and heat. Herds of bison roaming the plains left behind plenty of the free fuel. Pioneers called the dung "buffalo chips" or "meadow muffins." It was the only fuel they could find on the treeless prairie.

Huge turkey farms like this one have to deal with tons of manure.

burn it directly. The other is to let the manure rot, creating natural gas, and then burning the gas.

Chicken and turkey manure is best for direct burning. It's pretty dry and contains feathers and bedding as well as feces. The largest manure-burning electric plant in the world is in England. It burns about 463,000 tons (almost 420,000 metric tons) of chicken and turkey manure every year. That produces enough electricity for nearly eight thousand homes.

North Americans eat more than eight billion chickens and turkeys every year. Those birds leave behind about 13 million tons (almost 12 million metric tons) of manure. That manure could make enough electricity for the entire city of Miami, Florida!

Cattle and hog manure is much wetter than chicken and turkey manure. It would have to be dried before burning, which would be expensive. It's cheaper to turn cattle and hog manure into natural gas. We can burn the gas to heat homes or to make electricity.

Many cattle and hog farms are starting to produce electricity along with milk and meat. To make electricity, the manure goes into a big tank. The tank has a plastic cover. Wet manure enters the tank through a pipe in the

This manure tank is used to turn manure into natural gas.

bottom. New manure, added each day, pushes up the manure already in the tank. By the time manure reaches the top, it has turned into natural gas and liquid. It takes twenty to sixty days to turn manure into natural gas. The gas is piped off for burning, and the liquid is piped off separately for fertilizer.

Some farmers have electric generators on their farms. They make their own electricity from the natural gas they collect. Farmers use the electricity or sell it to their local power companies. Other farmers sell the gas itself to power companies.

There are more than one hundred million cattle and sixty million hogs in North America. They could become important sources of natural gas.

Sewage Solutions

Sewage is different from manure. It includes anything people or factories pour down the drain or flush down the toilet. Sewage contains

Recycling Milk

Another kind of trash from dairy farms is waste milk. Sometimes dirt gets into the milk. Dirty milk can't be sold for people to drink. But farmers can feed this milk to calves.

More often, the milk has germs in it that might make calves sick. In the past, farmers usually threw this milk away. But some farms have started recycling their waste milk by pasteurizing it (heating it to kill germs). Farmers can safely feed pasteurized milk to their calves.

Milk sold for people to drink is also pasteurized. But farm pasteurization doesn't kill enough germs to make waste milk safe for humans.

everything from feces and urine to trash and dirty water. It also contains dangerous chemicals and harmful metals. It's germy, slimy stuff.

We have to treat sewage to avoid spreading disease and poisoning the environment. Sewage treatment removes dangerous materials. The treatment separates the sewage into liquids and solids. These liquids and solids can be released back into the environment or reused.

Sludge is the solid stuff created by sewage treatment. Every year towns and cities in the United States have to get rid of more than 8 million tons (7,256,000 metric tons) of sludge. We bury about one-fifth of it in landfills, burn one-fifth, and use one-fifth in other ways. We spread the remaining two-fifths on farm fields as fertilizer.

Scientists disagree about whether sludge is safe to spread on fields. Some believe sewage treatment destroys most of the dangerous materials.

This worker talks on a walkie-talkie as he keeps on eye on operations at a sewage treatment plant.

They also believe that spreading the sludge thinly over large areas of land makes it less risky. Other scientists believe that sludge contains too many dangerous materials. They fear germs and poisons could get in our food through the soil or through water pumped from under the sludge.

Almost everyone agrees, though, that finding a safe use for sludge is better than burying it or burning it.

Zoo Poo

A few paper companies are recycling something very surprising. A company in England is one example. It's helping not only the environment, but also some local zookeepers. This company makes paper out of elephant dung from a nearby safari park (big zoo). The park is home to three Asian elephants.

Why make paper out of elephant dung? Asian elephants eat about 220 to 440 pounds (100 to 200 kg) of food per day. But their bodies use less than half of the food they eat. They poop out the rest. That means one elephant produces about 300 pounds (136 kg) of manure every day. That's a lot of manure for a zoo to get rid of!

The paper company picks up the manure from the zoo. The zoo workers are glad to donate it. At the paper mill, workers wash, boil, and dry the manure. When dry, it looks like dark brown cardboard. Workers then mix it with other recycled paper. The end product is a light-colored paper that makes fine stationery, notebooks, and cards.

This woman mixes elephant dung and paper pulp to make colored stationery at a recycling plant in Sri Lanka.

Does elephant dung paper stink? The paper makers say: No, all the smells and germs in the manure disappear during the washing, boiling, and drying. But most people who buy the paper give it a sniff anyway to make sure.

Pee Power

Scientists in Asia have invented a battery that runs on urine. The battery is a five-layer sandwich about the size of a credit card. In the center is a chemical-soaked paper. Thin layers of metal sandwich the paper. Two layers of plastic on the outside protect the inner layers.

Each end of the battery has a small slit. A drop of urine placed on the slit soaks into the paper. This starts a chemical reaction that makes electricity. One drop of human urine makes as much electricity as an AA battery for about ten minutes.

Urine-powered batteries can help medical workers in places where there's no electricity. The batteries can run testing machines. The batteries are cheap to make, and there'll never be a shortage of pee to run them!

chapter 3

E-waste and E-cycling

Electronic waste (e-waste) includes unwanted computers, cell phones, and other electronic machines and parts. Recycling e-waste is called e-cycling. E-cycling can mean giving away whole, working electronics for others to use. It can also mean collecting the valuable parts of electronics for other uses. (The useless parts go to landfills.)

North Americans throw away about 136,000 computers every day. Our landfills already contain about one hundred million computers and several hundred million phones, TVs, video games, and other electronics. No one knows how much more of

IT'S A FACT!

E-waste is piling up three times faster than ordinary trash. This is partly because electronics get out-of-date so quickly. Manufacturers constantly make better, faster, and more powerful machines. Everyone wants the latest model, so older models are hard to resell.

These computer monitors and other components are waiting to be recycled at a company in France.

this stuff is collecting dust on shelves and in closets. Sooner or later, it'll be shoved out the door with the rest of the trash. It all adds up to a mountain-size problem.

E-waste Is Different

E-waste is different from ordinary trash because electronics contain metals that can poison us. Lead and mercury are two especially dangerous metals in e-waste.

All computer monitors and many TV screens contain 2 to 8 pounds (about 1 to 3.6 kg) of lead in their glass. The lead traps harmful radiation (very fast-moving energy) given off by parts inside the monitor or TV. Even though lead can be dangerous, having lead in monitors and TVs is good while they're working.

The Four Rs
You can help cut down on all kinds of waste by following four simple rules:

1. Reduce. Use less. Buy only what you really need. Use up the products you buy. Buy products with less packaging.
2. Reuse. Upgrade your computer rather than buying a new one. Shop with bags from home. Borrow library magazines. Sell or donate useful things you don't want. Buy used things rather than new ones.
3. Recycle. Choose recyclable products. Recycle all the paper, plastic, aluminum, and glass you can. Compost yard and food waste for fertilizer.
4. Respond. Educate others about reducing, reusing, and recycling. Tell stores you prefer products with less packaging and things that are recycled or recyclable. Volunteer for community recycling efforts.

But when lead glass breaks or burns, lead can escape into the environment. Lead is very poisonous. In the human body, it can cause mental illness, kidney disease, and other serious kinds of sickness. When lead glass ends up in landfills, it often breaks, and tiny bits of lead can wash into water supplies and soil. When lead glass burns, the smoke carries lead into people's lungs.

E-waste also contains mercury, another very poisonous metal. Mercury causes some of the same health problems as lead. But mercury poisoning is more serious than lead poisoning. It can cause death much quicker.

E-waste contains more than thirty-five other metals too. These include gold, silver, nickel, and copper. Because of all these metals, many landfills no longer accept e-waste. Metals in electronics are hard to get rid of safely. But the metals are valuable if we can get them back. More and more companies are now e-cycling old electronics to collect the precious metals from them.

E-cycling Is Hard Work

One electronic machine may have only tiny amounts of each valuable metal. There's only one way to gather enough metal to sell. That's to take apart hundreds or thousands of machines. Then workers must sort and collect the tiny scraps of metal. This takes a lot of work and time. That's why North America ships two-thirds of its e-waste to other parts of the world.

An employee sifts through e-waste at a recycling facility in Bangalore, India.

In many countries, workers make much less money than North American workers do. It's cheaper for American companies to ship e-waste to these countries than to pay American workers to take the machines apart.

Shipping e-waste to other countries has its own problems, though. Many countries don't have laws to protect workers or the environment. Their workers may not know about the dangers of lead, mercury, or other harmful metals. They may let these poisons into their bodies, air, soil, or water without knowing it.

More and more states are passing laws to control e-waste. In California it's illegal to ship e-waste out of the country. In states where it's illegal to put e-waste in landfills, new companies are forming to collect the

This sign at an office supply store in Illinois tells customers that it can recycle their old electronics.

chapter 4

New Uses for Old Tires

North Americans throw away about three hundred million rubber tires every year. We repair about sixteen million and put them back on vehicles. We recycle about 233 million to other uses. We throw away or stockpile (store) the rest.

Stockpiling tires is bad for the environment because tires attract pests. Mosquitoes breed in rainwater trapped in tires. Mice and rats nest in tires. These pests spread dangerous diseases.

A lone person walks among millions of old tires at a California plant that burns the tires to make electricity.

Stockpiled tires also cause big problems if they catch fire. Burning tires give off dangerous gases, metals, and oil. One average car tire burning gives off more than 2 gallons (7.6 l) of oil. One million tires burning produce about 55,000 gallons (208,136 l) of oil. If the oil gets into water sources, it poisons the water and harms the environment.

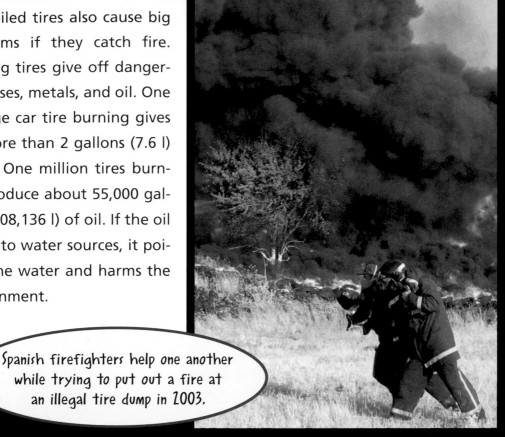

Spanish firefighters help one another while trying to put out a fire at an illegal tire dump in 2003.

Tire Fires

Tires are hard to start on fire, but once they start burning, tire fires are hard to put out. Water and firefighting foam don't help much. Bulldozers must push sand or dirt onto the tires to smother the flames. (Fire needs air to keep burning.)

In 1983 a stockpile of seven million tires in Virginia caught fire. The smoke spread out for 50 miles (80.5 km) and traveled to three states. It rose 3,000 feet (914.4 m) into the air. The fire burned for nine months.

People start most tire fires, either on purpose or by accident. Lightning can start a tire fire, but it happens very rarely.

Nearly one-tenth of U.S. scrap tires end up in landfills. That's about twenty-seven million tires every year. Tires cause problems in landfills. They take up lots of space. They also trap air underground because of their shape. Over time the tires can work their way to the surface, pulling up rotten garbage with them.

Most state laws say that tires must be shredded before going into landfills. In some places, tires go into monofills (landfills that allow only one type of trash). It's better to put tires in a monofill than to put them in an ordinary landfill or to stockpile them in the open. In a monofill, they're buried so they can't burn or attract pests. They may still rise to the surface, but at least they won't bring rotten garbage with them.

Finding new uses for scrap tires is even better than monofilling them. There are many good uses for old tires. Most of these uses require chopping the tires into crumb rubber. Recycling companies chop the tires down to different sizes for different uses.

This man holds crumb rubber from car tires. Manufacturers can use crumb rubber to make many products.

Rubber Roads

The biggest use of scrap tires is in building roads. Road workers can use chopped tires in many ways. The most common way is for asphalt rubber, which uses up about twelve million tires every year. Asphalt rubber combines crumb rubber with asphalt (a tarry black material). Workers heat them together to make road pavement. A two-lane road with an asphalt rubber surface 2 inches (5 cm) thick uses up four thousand tires per mile (per 1.6 km).

Asphalt rubber pavement lasts longer than regular asphalt. Asphalt gets brittle (hard and dry) and cracks over time. Water runs into the cracks and seeps under the road. This causes potholes and breaks up the road. Adding rubber helps the pavement bend and stretch instead of crack. Asphalt rubber roads don't need to be fixed as often as asphalt roads.

IT'S A FACT!
Roads made with rubber are quiet. People first noticed this in Belgium in 1981. Since then, tests have shown that cars make half as much noise on asphalt rubber roads as they do on other roads.

Another important road-building use of scrap tires is for roads in cold places. During the spring, melting snow and rain soak the ground, and extra water collects under roads. This water freezes and melts several times, breaking up the pavement. With a layer of shredded tires under the pavement, the water won't freeze. This saves a lot of time, work, and money fixing roads.

IT'S A FACT!
Rubber gives roads really good grip. Drivers can stop their cars in less time on asphalt rubber roads than on other roads.

People can use crumb rubber for other surfaces besides roads too. For example, floors made of recycled rubber can look like tile or stone. Rubber floors are comfortable to walk on and prevent slipping. They last for many years and can be recycled again. Crumb rubber can be combined with other materials to make sports fields and tracks. Rubber fields and tracks are easier to care for than grass or dirt.

Rubber mulch is another product made from crumb rubber. It makes a good playground surface because it's springy. When used in gardens, it holds moisture in the soil. Another use for rubber mulch is in horse arenas. Horse handlers like it because it's easy on horses' feet and legs.

But recycled rubber has some drawbacks. Rubber can get very hot in the sun—hot enough to melt sneaker soles! Some rubber sports fields and tracks use sprinkling systems to keep them cool. If rubber mulch catches on fire, the fire is hard to put out. Rubber mulch can contain poisonous metals and chemicals. These can get into soil or water.

This family plays on the swings in their yard. They used recycled rubber for the play area's surface.

Tires for Energy

Nearly half of all scrap tires in the United States are burned as fuel for businesses. Tires aren't good for heating homes. They must be burned in closed furnaces so their smoke and oil don't escape into the environment.

Tires can be burned either shredded or whole. Tires provide about the same amount of energy as oil. They provide more energy than coal and also burn cleaner than most coal.

Electric companies burn about thirty-four million tires every year. Businesses burn another seventeen million tires a year to heat their buildings. The tires heat water that's piped through the buildings. Some factories, such as cement and paper factories, burn tires for energy to run their machines.

This California power plant was the first U.S. plant to use whole tires for making electricity.

More Tire Inventions

More and more companies are finding new ways to use old tires. Tire bits can replace soil for many uses. They can fill in wet areas so workers can build roads through swamps. They can build up the sides of walls, roads, and bridges. They can re-place stone to help rainwater drain away from buildings. They even cover up garbage in land-fills that don't accept whole tires.

This road on Mayotte Island in the Indian Ocean runs alongside a dike (barrier) made of tires.

People are find-ing ways to recycle whole tires too. Car racetracks use them as crash barriers. Marinas hang them on docks as boat bumpers. Farmers use extra-large tires to hold hay bales in place for feeding animals. Families use them for planters, sandboxes, and swings.

The Osborne Reef Disaster

Artificial reefs (undersea structures) provide homes for fish and other sea ani-mals, such as barnacles, corals, sponges, and oysters. Sunken vehicles and pieces of torn-down buildings make good artificial reefs. In 1974 a company used old tires to enlarge Osborne Reef off the coast of Fort Lauderdale, Florida. The U.S. Navy and many private boats helped. A tire company lent tools for the project.

Workers dropped two million tires bundled with steel clips into the sea. But no an-imals ever moved in. The clips broke, and the tires separated. They started to drift, crashing into and hurting natural coral and rock reefs. Hurricanes tossed thousands of tires onto Florida beaches. No one knows how far some have traveled.

In 2007 a cleanup of this failed project began.

chapter 5

Turning Crude Stuff into Crude Oil

Garbage has less value than anything on earth. In fact, garbage is so worthless, it's actually expensive to keep it around. It costs billions of dollars a year to take care of something that nobody wants! To solve this problem, scientists are working on ways to turn garbage into oil, one of the most valuable materials on our planet.

Crude oil is a dark liquid found far underground. People refine it to make gasoline, fuel oil, plastic, fabric, fertilizer, and thousands of other products. Crude oil is so valuable, it's sometimes called black gold.

Some crude oil is found under the ocean floor. This oil rig pumps oil and sends it through an undersea pipeline to oil refineries.

The main chemical building blocks of crude oil are carbon and hydrogen. These are the main building blocks of all living things. Scientists believe the earth's heat and pressure on dead plants and animals buried underground formed crude oil. The earth takes a long time to make crude oil naturally. That's why crude oil isn't a renewable energy source.

Garbage is made of the same things as crude oil. It's mostly dead plants and animals in the form of paper, leaves, food, plastic, rubber, leather, cloth, and wood. What if we could put heat and pressure on garbage to make crude oil? What if we could do it in hours rather than thousands of years? If we could do it fast enough, we could turn piles of our most worthless junk into barrels of our most valuable liquid.

Several universities and businesses are trying out different ways of making crude oil from garbage. One idea is turning hog manure to oil in a way that removes all the smell. Another idea is turning manure and vegetable waste into oil. Some cities have proposed turning sewage sludge into oil. If these ideas work, crude oil will become a renewable energy source.

Oil from Animals

One business in Missouri is already making oil from garbage. It's next-door to one of the biggest turkey processing plants in the country. The plant processes thirty thousand turkeys every day. That creates 200 tons (181.4 metric tons) of waste a day. The waste includes skin, bones, fat, intestines, organs, feet, heads, feathers, and blood.

This gruesome waste goes into a huge grinder first. The grinder finely chops everything up and adds water. The waste comes out a grayish

Construction on this garbage-to-fuel plant (*top*) in Missouri began in late 2006. Other similar plants have also opened, including one in Pennsylvania that turns waste into clean fuel (*bottom*).

brown liquid. This liquid flows through a series of tanks that heat it, put pressure on it, then cool it. This breaks down the turkey parts and changes them into oil. The heating time is about fifteen minutes at about 500°F (260°C). The whole process from raw garbage to crude oil takes about two hours.

From 1 ton (0.9 metric ton) of turkey waste, the plant can make 600 pounds (272.2 kg) of high-grade crude oil similar to diesel fuel. The plant can make up to 21,000 gallons (79,470 l) of oil a day. The oil can be refined more to make gasoline or kerosene. The oil-making process also creates useful things like natural gas and fertilizer. The used water is recycled back into the plant.

The Missouri garbage-to-fuel plant opened in 2004. The next year, Missouri's governor ordered the plant to close because people complained about its smell. The plant quickly took steps to control the smell and started up again. Plant officials say it costs about as much to make oil in their plant as it does to explore and drill for natural crude oil, without hurting the environment.

This garbage-to-fuel process kills all the germs in the garbage. It also removes or grinds up metals, sharp objects, and other difficult items fairly easily. That means this process could be used to make oil from household waste, medical waste, hazardous waste, e-waste, tires, and sewage sludge without danger to people.

If just the farm waste produced in the United States could be turned into oil, it would create four billion barrels of oil per year. That's about how much oil we buy from other countries every year. We'd need to build garbage-to-oil plants all over the country, which would take a lot of work and money. But many scientists and government leaders believe the change would be worth the effort.

Oil from Plastic

Plants in Japan and Great Britain have been turning used plastic into fuel since the 1990s. Like the garbage-to-oil process, this process also uses grinding, heat, and pressure. Unlike other kinds of plastic recycling, the plastic-to-oil process doesn't require sorting or washing. It can use all sorts of plastic—even plastics that aren't otherwise recyclable.

A plastic-to-oil plant can process up to 22 tons (20 metric tons) of plastic per day. That produces about 5,000 gallons (18,921 l) of oil. This high-grade oil works in any engine that can burn artificial fuel. Some

Hazardous Waste

Some kinds of trash are too dangerous to put into ordinary landfills. This type of trash is called hazardous waste. Household hazardous waste includes paint, cleaning liquids, motor oil, batteries, and pesticides. Industrial hazardous waste includes many chemicals used in factories and mining. Hazardous waste must go to special landfills that keep the dangerous materials away from the environment.

Medical waste is a special kind of hazardous waste. It includes things that have blood on them, such as needles and other medical tools. It also includes parts of people's bodies removed in surgery. Blood and flesh contain germs that could spread diseases. Medical waste must be burned or sterilized (to kill germs) before going to a landfill.

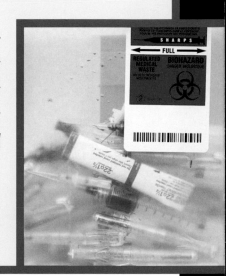

Medical waste, such as these used syringes, is a kind of hazardous waste.

plants have electric generators built into them, so they produce electrical power as well as oil.

The Nature of Recycling

Oil buried under the earth is a result of natural recycling. Thousands of years ago, the earth recycled dead plants and animals to form oil. Recycling is an important part of nature.

Humans are doing the same thing. People are turning unwanted materials into oil and other useful things. We're learning the importance of reducing, reusing, and recycling. When we recycle, we help nature. And when we help nature, we help ourselves.

Glossary

aluminum: a lightweight, silvery metal often used for drink cans

bale: a big, tightly bound bundle

compost: a mixture of rotted leaves, vegetables, or manure used to enrich soil and help plants grow

crude oil: a thick, oily liquid found underground, used to make gasoline, fuel oil, plastic, and many other products

dung: solid waste from animals; poop

excrement: solid waste from animals and people; poop

feces: solid waste from animals and people; poop

fiberfill: artificial stuffing used as insulation in clothes, quilts, pillows, and cushions

flame-retardant: hard to burn

generator: a machine that produces electricity

hazardous waste: dangerous trash that needs special handling to be safely thrown away

industrial waste: trash from factories and mining

infrared sensor: a tool that detects differences in light that human eyes can't see

landfill: a place where garbage is buried or contained so it won't harm the surrounding environment

materials recovery facility: a plant that processes trash so it can be used again; a recycling center

medical waste: trash from medical clinics and hospitals, much of which contains blood and other germy material

monofill: a landfill that accepts only one kind of trash

nutrient: any material that people, animals, or plants need to stay strong and healthy

pasteurize: to heat a liquid to a temperature high enough to kill germs

polyester: a kind of cloth made from artificial plastic thread

polyethylene terephthalate (PETE): a kind of plastic used mostly to make cloth, insulation, and bottles and jars for foods and drinks

radiation: tiny parts that break off from materials, causing harmful, very fast-moving rays of energy. Radiation can't be seen, heard, or felt, but can cause serious illness.

recycle: to process used or unwanted items so they can be made into new products

recycling center: a plant that processes trash for reuse; materials recovery facility

renewable energy: energy from sources that can't be used up, such as wind, waves, or sunlight, or that can be replaced, such as plants and manure

rubber mulch: a ground cover made from chopped or shredded tires

sewage: liquid and solid waste carried away in drains and toilets

sewage sludge: solid matter left over after sewage treatment

spinneret: a machine with many holes in it, through which liquid is forced to form strands that harden and can be twisted into thread

sterilized: cleaned so thoroughly that all germs are killed

urine: liquid waste from animals and people; pee

X-ray: an invisible kind of energy that can pass through solid objects

Selected Bibliography

American Plastics Council. "Plastic Packaging Resins." *American Chemistry Council Plastics Division Learning Center.* 2007.
http://www.americanchemistry.com/s_plastics/bin.asp?CID=1102&DID=4645&DOC=FILE.PDF (February 27, 2007).

Dubanowitz, Alexander. "Design of a Materials Recovery Facility (MRF) for Processing the Recyclable Materials of New York City's Municipal Solid Waste." *Columbia University Earth Engineering Center.* May 2000.
http://www.seas.columbia.edu/earth/dubanmrf.pdf (November 28, 2006).

Halweil, Brian. "Plastic Bags." *Worldwatch Institute Publications: Good Stuff?* 2006.
http://www.worldwatch.org/node/1499 (November 27, 2006).

Lee, Ki Bang. "Urine-Activated Paper Batteries for Biosystems." *Journal of Micromechanics and Microengineering.* August 15, 2005.
http://www.iop.org/EJ/abstract/0960-1317/15/9/S06 (December 7, 2006).

Lemley, Brad. "Anything into Oil." *Discover.* May 2003, 50–57.

National Association for PET Container Resources. *NAPCOR Website.* 2004.
http://www.napcor.com (November 29, 2006).

National Recovery Technologies. "High-Speed Identification and Sorting of Plastic Resin Flake for Recycling." *Small Business Innovation Research Success Stories.* November 27, 2006. http://es.epa.gov/ncer/sbir/success/pdf/highspeed.pdf (December 5, 2006).

Royte, Elizabeth. "E-gad!" *Smithsonian.* August 2005, 82–86.

Royte, Elizabeth. *Garbage Land: On the Secret Trail of Trash.* New York: Little, Brown and Company, 2005.

Tufts University. "History and Statistics of U.S. Waste Production and Recycling." *Tufts Recycles! Facts Pages.* N.d. http://www.tufts.edu/tuftsrecycles/USstats.htm (November 27, 2006).

USC Trojan Family Magazine. "Alumni Profile: Gary Anderson." *Alumni News.*
   Summer 2000.
   http://www.usc.edu/dept/pubrel/trojan_family/summer00/alumninews/AP_
   Anderson.html (February 27, 2007).

U.S. Environmental Protection Agency. "Recycling." *U.S. Environmental Protection*
   Agency Municipal Solid Waste. October 23, 2006.
   http://www.epa.gov/epaoswer/non-hw/muncpl/recycle.htm (November
   27–December 7, 2006).

Donald, Rhonda Lucas. *Recycling*. New York: Children's Press, 2002. This book describes waste management, explains why recycling is important, and offers some new ways to recycle.

EPA Student Center. http://www.epa.gov/students. This U.S. Environmental Protection Agency (EPA) website provides stories, games, puzzles, and activities. It also links to a large network of other websites for students and teachers.

Ganeri, Anita. *Something Old, Something New: Recycling*. Chicago: Heinemann Library, 2005. This book uses a fun approach to show how people can help our planet by recycling.

How Products Are Made. http://www.madehow.com. This searchable website is loaded with articles describing how products are made and used.

Inskipp, Carol. *Reducing and Recycling Waste*. Milwaukee: Gareth Stevens Publishing, 2005. This book describes the many environmental problems caused by waste. It also suggests ways to help solve these problems by reducing waste and recycling.

Martin, Laura. *Recycled Crafts Box*. North Adams, MA: Storey Publishing, 2003. This book shows kids how to use recycled paper, plastic, metal, and fabric for craft projects. Each section describes how the materials are made and how they can be recycled.

NAPCOR'S Kids Corner. http://www.napcor.com/kidscorner.htm. This website provides information, activities, and downloads about PETE recycling. It also offers free samples of recycled PETE for classroom use.

Parker, Steve. *Green Files: Waste and Recycling*. Chicago: Heinemann Library, 2004. This book shows how half of household trash can be recycled. It also discusses new ways of using old cars.

Ross, Michael Elsohn. *Junk Lab*. Minneapolis: Millbrook Press, 2003. This book in the You Are the Scientist series shows kids different experiments that reuse common household garbage items, such as plastic containers.

Index

Photo Acknowledgments

Photographs are used with the permission of: Photodisc Royalty Free by Getty Images, pp. 5, 37, background image on pp. 1 and even pages 2 – 28, © Reuters/CORBIS, p. 6; © age fotostock/SuperStock, pp. 9, 10 (left), 36; © J. King-Holmes/Photo Researchers, Inc., p. 10 (right); © Pegasus/Visuals Unlimited, p. 11; © Roger Wright/Stone/Getty Images, p. 12; Courtesy of relan, LLP, p. 14; Courtesy Re Created Design, p. 15; © Jim Richardson/CORBIS, p. 17; © Justin Sullivan/Getty Images, p. 19; © Nigel Cattlin/Visuals Unlimited, p. 20; © Lester Lefkowitz/Photographer's Choice/Getty Images, p. 22; © Rob Elliott/AFP/Getty Images, p. 23; © Bisson Bernard/CORBIS SYGMA, p. 25; © Manjunath Kiran/epa/CORBIS, p. 27; © Tim Boyle/Getty Images, p. 28; © Jose Azel/Aurora/Getty Images, p. 30; © Christophe Simon/AFP/Getty Images, p. 31; © AP Photo/Dan Loh, p. 32; © AP Photo/Scott Martin, p. 34; © AP Photo, p. 35; © AP Photo/Joel West Ray, p. 39 (top); © AP Photo/Mark Stehle, p. 39 (bottom); © Dana Neely/Photographer's Choice/Getty Images, p. 40.

Front cover: © Photodisc Royalty Free by Getty Images, background, bottom; © Justin Sullivan/Getty Images, top; © Joe Raedle/Getty Images, right.

About the Author

Charlotte Wilcox is the author of many nonfiction books for young readers, including *Bald Eagles; The Iroquois; Mummies & Their Mysteries; Mummies, Bones & Body Parts,* and *The Seminoles.*